Building Strong Families with Proverbs

by John L. Kachelman, Jr.

ISBN: 0-89137-141-9

Contents

Introduction

Building Strong Families With Proverbs!

About the Use of this Material. . .

This material was originally prepared for the 1992 Freed-Hardeman University Bible Lectureship. The theme of that year's lectures focused upon the family. It was my pleasure to study through **The Book of Proverbs** and discuss how God expects us to build strong families by utilizing the inspired counsel of Proverbs. The study was most profitable and the reception of the lectures was most humbling. Bennie Whitehead, of Quality Publications, suggested that the notes and transparencies be made available so that Churches could incorporate the Proverbs' sage counsel into a class study. This is the result of his suggestion. These four studies can easily fill a 13 week quarter of study (each study can be so divided to fill three periods of study and the final period can be used as a summary of the previous 12 lessons).

I want to express my appreciation for the invitation of **Freed-Hardeman University** to present these lectures. As an alumnus of that institution I appreciate the commitment to adhere to God's inspired directions in every aspect of life. The 1992 focus on the biblical teachings about the family is reflective of the administration, faculty, and staff who have committed themselves to the heavenly Father's will. I urge all who use this study series to order the 1992 Lectureship book. Not only will you find additional material on the studies in this book but you will possess a valuable volume that addresses many aspects of the family. Audio tapes of each lecture are available and should provide additional resources for these lessons. I have included details for ordering these items in the bibliography of resources.

The transparencies contained in this study can easily be made with any copier. Their appearance is enhanced if the teacher will take a few minutes and add color by using any permanent marker (I have found it best to color the reverse side for some transparency images will be erased by the marker.). I cannot claim credit for the illustrations used. These have been "clipped" from bulletins, newspapers, and other sources of public materials. I wish I knew the artists. These unknowns have added to the effective teaching of God's Word.

The study notes list a number of texts. It is suggested that the teacher give attention to these and specifically explain how they apply to the topic under study.

I have included a bibliography of resource materials which have been useful. Some are quoted within the notes. Others have offered ideas and thoughts to the series.

The urgency of Christians building strong families is underscored by this observation:

> *The dissolution of the family is at the root of nearly all the social problems afflicting contemporary American society. The high rate of divorce is making emotional cripples out of children at all levels of society. And the children of divorce become divorced themselves at much higher rates than others. Crime, drug abuse, alcoholism, mental illness, venereal disease, low educational achievement, lack of job-related skills, inability to function well on jobs, all of these things—and many more—can have their causes traced to the disintegration of the traditional family.*
>
> [***Homosexuality And The Natural Law,*** Harry V. Jaffa. Center for the Study of the Natural Law: The Clairmont Institute, 4650 Arrow Highway, Suite D-6, Montclair, CA 91763, p. 38-39].

May these study notes help build strong families who will serve the Almighty with determined resolve! (Joshua 24:15b)!

The Family's Foundation — Marriage

John L. Kachelman, Jr.

I. Introduction of the study series, "Building a Strong Family!"

A. Introduce the Book of Proverbs
   1. ***Show Transparency 1/2*** - "Outline of Proverbs"
   2. Proverbs is vastly different from other biblical books. Nearly two-thirds of the 915 verses are short, pithy sayings rather than an on-going narrative.
   3. Here is one of the most quoted and mis-quoted books of the entire Bible. Famous quotations, worldly wisdom, or common sensical thoughts have been erroneously attributed to Proverbs [i.e. "Every tub must sit on its bottom." Or "Hell hath no fury like a woman"].
   4. Authorship is a simple matter:
      a. 1:1 - King Solomon compiled the majority of the proverbs (cf. 1 Kings 4:32).
      b. 22:17-24:34 - words of unknown wise men.
      c. Proverbs 25-29 - King Hezekiah's men were inspired to write these.
      d. Proverbs 30 - the words of Agur.
      e. Proverbs 31 - the words of King Lemuel.
   5. Value of Proverbs today
      a. The timeless truths are desperately needed in our day of intellectual madness! (Proverbs 11:7,22; 10:27).
      b. Its practical wisdom is needed in our time of practical ignorance! (Proverbs 26:17; 28:13).
      c. Thomas Campbell believed Proverbs was so valuable that he had his children memorize the entire book.
      d. It is valuable - its wisdom addresses every aspect of life: work, habits, speech, thoughts, associations, etc. There is NOT ONE aspect of human life that is not discussed in Proverbs!
   6. Briefly discuss the teaching methods of Proverbs.
      a. ***Transparency 1/2a*** (26:3,8; 27:10b).
      b. ***Transparency 1/2b*** (3:1b-2; 6:27,28; 7:1; 4:3-9; 7:6-23; 3:13; 5:15).

B. Our focus upon this marvelous book is specific - the Family Relationship. We will discover how to use Proverb's wisdom to build a **STRONG FAMILY.** Use ***Transparency A*** to give an overview of the study series. Proverbs is certainly a book that, when used, will build a very STRONG FAMILY!

C. The need for this series is evident.
   1. The "family" in America has undergone revolutionary changes in the last 40-50 years. Documentation is easily found and is currently revealing problems of tragic proportions.
   2. ***Transparency 1/1*** - Here is just one illustration that aptly summarizes the problem.
      a. "Uprootedness" - In many sections of our nation the "stable" lifestyle has vanished. Families are becoming more transient and that has repercussions on family values.
      b. Divorce has always threatened the Family but in our modern time it has grown into an enormous monster. "Blended Families" are redefining morals and values.
      c. Secular schools have replaced the home as the center of life's education. Children seldom are "taught" anything at home. Consequently the interaction of parent with child, through which values were transmitted, has ceased.
      d. Parental apathy is evident in the Bible Class Programs. Parents expect Bible Classes (and the Elders, Youth Minister; etc.), to teach their children basic religious facts.

e. The exodus of full-time mothers from the home to the work place has resulted in children being cared for by institutional means which are incapable of supplying the maternal nourishing critical to a child's development. ***Note:*** Proverbs 31:16 cannot justify the neglect of motherly responsibilities. The "worthy woman" worked but not to the extent that her children were denied a caring mother who was "at home" (31:27).

3. It is undeniable that the Family is in trouble. We need to correct this problem. The Book of Proverbs is an excellent resource for such correction!

D. The series will develop and explain these points (***Transparency A***).
1. The Family's Foundation - MARRIAGE
2. The Family's Founders - PARENTING
3. The Family's Fruits - CHILDREN
4. The Family's Filigree - TRAITS

II. THE FAMILY'S FOUNDATION - MARRIAGE

A. Before we look at any other aspect of the family, we must consider marriage. This is the starting point!
1. Ordained of God in Eden's bliss, this divine institution has taken severe blows over the past years.
2. Marriage has been revamped and ravaged until it is far from God's holy design!
3. ***Transparency 1/3*** - The sanctity of marriage is of paramount interest as Solomon writes. Four eternal truths about marriage will help the marriage union be strong.
   a. Marriage is good because it is a "GIFT" from God (Genesis 2:22b). It is good because God ordained it; Jesus affirmed it in Cana (John 2); Paul acclaimed it with inspiration (Ephesians 5). Proverbs 19:14 - this "gift" is better than anything our fathers can bequeath us!
   b. Marriage ennobles - "CROWN" (12:4). An aura of royalty!
   c. Marriage will bring RICH TREASURE (21:20). It is a delicacy likened to "oil." Oil was valuable (hygiene, medicine, fuel, cooking, etc.) Cf. 24:3,4.
   d. Marriage deserves FIDELITY (5:1-23). Failure to guard the union brings dire results: loss of honor/respect, wealth, bitter regret. Fidelity practiced brings great joy (5:15-20). Here Solomon urges his son not to mere steel-willed commitment, but to a single-hearted, impassioned affection for his wife!
   e. ***Note:*** A marriage founded upon these qualities will be strong!

B. But this beauty is often marred. Proverbs pinpoints **Five Foes of Marrige.**
1. 31:3-9 - Lemuel's mother admonished her son to be wary of the dangers of sex and selfishness.
2. Solomon's counsel specified three particulars that will weaken and destroy a strong marriage.
   a. ***Transparency 1/3a - ADULTERY.*** The frank discussion tells us that this is not a problem novel to us (5:1-7:27).
      1) Adultery is described as a shattering, soul-destroying act. It can rarely be kept secret. When it is hid it grinds on the spirit and burdens the soul. When made public it brings shame, humiliation, and loss of respect (5:9-10).
      2) The temptation is great (5:3; 7:21). But the end is fatal (7:24-27; 20:17; 22:14).
      3) **5:23 - 3 Great Truths About Adultery** are seen here.
         a) Death is the end of immorality.
         b) Rebellion against instructions leads to a mistake from which recovery is hard.
         c) One should be "intoxicated" with the love of a spouse (v.19), not an immoral lover (v.20). When this is not practiced, one is "overdosed" with great folly! "Go astray" is from the same verb as "exhilarated" in v. 19,20.
      4) Solomon's admonition is seldom heard today! Strong families do not ignore the danger of adultery!

      Our best choices are still our own partners, with whom we need to keep affections alive, courtships strong, passions kindled. Whatever attracted us to each other in the first place can be recalled and experienced afresh. Water is not sweeter elsewhere nor grass greener. Not as long as God is in heaven and our ways "are before the eyes of the Lord." God has called us to be loyal to each other in order to portray to the whole human family how deathlessly loyal He is to us. Heeding that call or not heeding it has consequences that are nothing less than cosmic. [Hubbard, ***Proverbs***].

   b. ***Transparency 1/3b - Contentious Attitudes***
      1) Here are oft read proverbs - 19:13; 21:9; 25:24; 21:19. Usually they are referred to in jest.

2) But Solomon is not jesting - here is a serious problem in marriage that affects the entire family! Note two of these references:
   a) **25:24** - A person that picks a fight as a way of life is unfit for marriage. S/He quarrels about every decision - who, what, how, and why! Solomon says that isolation, even though uncomfortable, is preferred. "Corner" - probably a tiny attic room used for storage. Such a person will never change from his/her commitment to nagging!
   b) **27:15,16** - Such a spouse perpetually repeats in the quarrelsome way. "Restrain" - to put in a hiding place where s/he will not disturb anyone is about as successful as grabbing the wind or preventing oil from escaping your clenched fist!
   c) Compulsive contention is hard to live with. You cannot stand it and you cannot stop it! Solomon says beware of this before you marry!
3) ***Transparency 1/3d*** - Proverbs gives us wise counsel on how we are to avoid marrige with such a contentious person. It is a positive exhortation to marry someone with three wonderful qualities.
   a) **17:9** - Look for one who is able to keep silent about your mistakes. "Seeks love" - pursues the way to show love and maintain friendship.
   b) **21:19** - Isolation is the better choice if the forbearance of 17:9a is not found!
   c) **13:3** - Find one who "guards" the mouth. **15:2** explains how this is done - "studies" literally meditates on a response before speaking (cf. 17:28).

c. **Transparency 1/3c - Domineering Attitudes.** Such a spouse will affect one's entire being. **12:4** - "bones" can stand for the entire self which is weak (i.e. "Rest my weary bones"). The contrast is found in **14:30** where self-control is viewed. Such a perverse attitude destroys the emotional life of the spouse and ruins marriage (14:1).

C. Note now the **"Marriage Mates"** as described in Proverbs.

1. ***The Wife - Transparency 1/4***
   a. **"Excellent" (12:4; 31:10).** This includes such ideas as strength of character, ability, merit, and reputation. She has integrity that sets her far apart from the immoral woman (22:14).
   b. **"Wise" (14:1).** Literally this is "womanly wisdom." She is wise in performing her role; utilizing her feminine charms given to her by God. She uses her womanly wisdom to build her "house" - i.e. those who live together. This "wisdom" enables the home to offer stability.
      Note: Here is a vital point - the home's stability often hinges upon the woman. Her behavior can make the ultimate difference between its welfare and its destruction! (cf. 1 Timothy 5:14; Titus 2:4).
   c. **"Prudent" (19:14).** Refers to her ability to make decisions. She is wise in choosing options that will benefit the family. Synonym: clever, effective.
   d. **"Worthy" (31:10-31). "Virtuous."** Her entire life, work, marriage, and children reveal her as possessing a reputation of godliness, responsibility, and loyalty.
   e. **"Good" (18:22). "Thing"** has been supplied and is objected to by some, but the meaning is clear - the woman who marries and guides her married life by Proverbs is simply "Good." ***Note:*** Nothing in Scripture ever tells us that a quarrelsome wife is a gift from God!

   "Man being made best and most excellent of all, Eve's being made after Adam, and out of Adam, puts an honor upon that sex as the glory of man. . . If man is the head, she is the crown, a crown to her husband, the crown of the visible creation. Man was dust refined but the woman was dust double-refined, once removed further from the earth. [Matthew Henry on Genesis 2:21-25].

2. ***The Husband - Transparency 1/5.*** Almost nothing is said about how a husband should treat his wife. But the general principles, urged upon the behavior of the man, apply in his home as well as in society.
   a. He is to **enjoy marriage** (5:18; Ecclesiastes 9:9).
   b. He is to **speak with affection** (19:22; 17:14; 14:22b).
   c. He is to **provide support/income** (10:5).
   d. He is **the "head"** - he should initiate teaching, training, exemplify respect to his wife, provide a godly example in all things. "Husband" - literally from Anglo-Saxon meaning "band of the family."
   e. **He expresses thanks** for the "GOOD Thing" that God has given him (18:22). Seeing the wife as God's unique gift, he will shower her with the love God expects to be found in marriage.

The STRONG Family According To Proverbs Has These Particular Traits:

The Family's FOUNDATION
(Marriage)

The Family's FOUNDERS
(Parenting)

The Family's FRUITS
(Children)

The Family's FILIGREE
(Uniqueness)

[Transparency A]

The Withering Away of the Family

Five reasons why the modern family structure has been undermind.

1. "Uprootedness"

2. Ease of divorce
   {no permanence}

3. School replacing home

4. Bible Classes replacing home

5. Public employment of women

[From E. Trueblood, THE RECOVERY OF FAMILY LIFE.]

[Transparency 1/1]

An Outline of Proverbs

I. Instructions to seek Wisdom
{1:1-9:18}

II. Proverbs of Solomon
{10:1-22:16}

III. Words of the Wise
{22:17-24:34}

IV. Proverbs of Solomon through
Hezekiah's Scribes {25:1-29:27}

V. Words of Agur
{30:1-33}

VI. Words of Lemuel
{31:1-31}

[Transparency 1/2]

PROVERBIAL SAYINGS

Three different ways are used in Proverbs to depict wisdom or folly in everyday choices.

SIMILARITIES

Similar ideas are placed back-to-back so that one line [sometimes two] illustrates the main point. See 26:3; 25:12,14,25,28.

SIMILE

Use of "like" or "as" to express the link between the illustration and the main point. See 26:8; 10:1,11,18; 27:8,19.

SUPERIORITIES

Beginning with "Better" to demonstrate how wise behavior, even in humble circumstances, outweighs power or affluence when folly is their price. See 15:16,17; 12:9; 16:8,19; 17:1; 19:1; 27:4,10b.

[Transparency 1/2a]

TEACHING TECHNIQUES of Israel's Sages

Admonitions
3:1b-2; 1:15-16

Rhetorical Questions
6:27,28; 30:4

Calls to Attention
1:8-9; 5:1; 7:1

Reflections on Experiences
4:3-9

Personal Observations
7:6-23; Ecclesiastes 1:13,14,16

Beatitudes
3:13-14

Allegory
5:15-23

[Transparency 1/2b]

The Sanctity of Marriage

Marriage is A GIFT (19:14)

Marriage ENNOBLES (12:4)

Marriage Brings TREASURE (21:20)

Marriage Deserves FIDELITY (5:1-23)

[Transparency 1/3]

Destructive Elements in Marriage

1. Adultery

Contentious Attitudes

Domineering Attitudes

[Transparency 1/3a]

Destructive Elements in Marriage

1. Adultery

Contentious Attitudes

Domineering Attitudes

[Transparency 1/3b]

Destructive Elements in Marriage

1. Adultery
2. Contentious Attitudes

Domineering Attitudes

[Transparency 1/3c]

Wisdom's 3 Imperatives for Marriage

FORGIVENESS
{Proverbs 17:9}

FORBEARANCE
{Proverbs 21:19}

SENSITIVITY
{Proverbs 12:18-23; 13:3; 15:1,2; etc.}

[Transparency 1/3d]

The Wife

According to Proverbs

"Excellent"
{Proverbs 12:4}

"Wise"
{14:1}

"Prudent"
{19:14}

"Worthy"
{Proverbs 31:10-31}

"Good Thing"
{Proverbs 18:22}

[Transparency 1/4]

The Husband

According to Proverbs

He "enjoys" marriage
{Proverbs 5:18;
Ecclesiastes 9:9}

He Speaks with
affection {19:22}

He provides support
{Proverbs 6:6ff; 10:4}

He is the "HEAD"
{Proverbs 1:8; etc.}

He expresses thanks for his wife
{Proverbs 18:22}

[Transparency 1/5]

The Family's Founders — Parenting

John L. Kachelman, Jr.

I. Review previous lecture. Use *Transparency A* to show the class the scope of the lecture series.

A. Proverbs is a book dedicated to parents. The entire Book is a rich resource from which parents can glean an exceptional training in child-rearing.

B. According to Scripture, a **STRONG FAMILY** has the benefit of BOTH father and mother. This is the divinely designed balance of a home - both working together (22:6). ***Note:*** The tragedy that is sweeping America today is the failure of families to possess this "balance" of 1:8. Single parent families are growing at a disturbing rate. Millions of children are doomed to an unbalanced home.

II. Scriptural parenting for a STRONG FAMILY can be outlined in 3 main points.

A. The Father's Role

B. The Mother's Role

C. The Assurance of parenting

III. *Transparency 2/1 - The Father's Role*

A. The father is viewed in Proverbs as a strong force within the family (17:6b).
1. The "glory" refers to a headdress that marked people as worthy of respect and admiration.
2. Fathers who are strong bring dignity to their families. Such have children who "glory" in them - they brag about their "Daddy"!
3. This "strength" is also evident in the way the father approaches family decisions, corrects children's behavior, and treats his wife.
4. Such "strength" provides the child with a steady anchor even when "Dad" has long since died!

B. Fathers nurture a strong family by accepting responsibility for directing the family. The "wise" father will choose the righteous way for his family (cf. Joshua 24:15b; Genesis 18:19). The responsible father will direct his family to "safety" (lit. "salvation"). The focus of 11:14 is upon choices. Fathers must train children to make right choices! ***Note:*** 1 Kings 12:8 where Rehoboam failed to follow his father's advice and has become known as a great Fool!

C. Fathers must DISCIPLINE children.
1. This is a frequent command: 10:13; 12:1; 13:24; 18:21; 19:18; 20:30; 22:6,15; 23:13,14; 26:3; 29:15,17.
2. We will discuss this fully in Lecture #3. For now, we quickly note these facts - ***Transparency 2/2.***
   a. Rebellion results when discipline is neglected (17:25). It is tragic when a child brings "grief" instead of joy (17:21; cf. 10:1; 15:5,20; 19:13).
   b. Discipline will correct error and save the child from calamity. Solomon uses metaphors to reveal the safety found in discipline - lamp, light, safe road (6:23). The contrast in 15:31,32 reveals that when discipline is neglected the internal self will find tragic fruits.
   c. Discipline reveals parental concern/love (3:11,12). Often the parent who corrects a child is viewed as harsh and unloving, but not so! (13:24).
   d. ***Note:*** A father's punishment does not necessarily involve physical spanking. Often words are sufficient (29:15 - "reproof;" cf. 17:10; 18:21; 19:25).
3. The practice of discipline is not pleasant. But the father MUST see that it is done. Without it there is only tragedy awaiting. See 19:18 - The exhortation here is for parents to correct a child while that correction will be effective. The proverb tells us that there will come a time when foolishness has taken root and change is impossible. The greatest tragedy only awaits,

total "destruction." Parents who refuse to correct a child are giving a virtual death sentence instead of "love." Parents have but a few brief years "while there is hope." We must not waste any of that precious time!

D. ***Transparency 2/1*** - Fathers must guide their families in righteous living. 12:28 emphasizes why fathers must do this. Deuteronomy 6:6-9 explains how this guidance takes place. This important text (Deuteronomy 6) will be discussed in the last study. ***Note Transparency 2/3*** for specific topics that the father of a STRONG FAMILY will discuss with children.

E. ***Transparency 2/1*** - Fathers must leave a godly inheritance for their children (13:22). Not only will the father of a STRONG FAMILY have something of material value to pass onto future generations, but he will leave behind invaluable Truth (Genesis 18:19). Solomon says at least 2 generations will be beneficiaries of the godly father!

F. Fathers must provide strength for their family when it struggles with troubles (24:10). Adversity tests the family. But the father should stand fast - not idle, disheartened, falling apart, or giving up. He must show depths of character and confidence of faith! (Matthew 13:21).

IV. *The Mother's Role*

A. ***Transparency 2/4*** - Before we focus upon the mother, look at how Proverbs treats women.
   1. The book was written to a man as a guidebook for successful living. It is significant to note that discussions regarding women occupy large sections. And from these sections, those focusing upon mothers are overwhelming!
   2. ***Transparency 2/4*** - In regard to women, Proverbs makes 3 general points
      a. Women are uniquely mothers! They are created to nurture, bear, and raise children (23:25). ***Note:*** This is one argument being made against women in combat!
      b. Womanhood is exalted! Whether as a wife, daughter, or mother, Solomon urges men to view the female as an exquisite gift of precious quality! (31:29; 5:18; 19:14).
      c. Men must honor women (12:4; 18:22; 31:10).
   3. Read comments on ***Transparency 2/4.***

B. ***Transparency 2/5*** - The last chapter of Proverbs is probably the best known - "The Worthy Woman." It is a marvelous discussion of the "words of King Lemuel that his mother taught him" (31:1). Many sermons, articles, songs, and poems find their source in this marvelous text. Look at Proverbs 31 and focus upon its message regarding the mother of a STRONG FAMILY.
   1. Motherhood is an honored role! (31:10).
      a. The rhetorical question demands a response that emphasizes a rare quality.
      b. "Rubies" ["Jewels" NASB] links her to "wisdom" (8:11) and sets this woman above that quality.
      c. Motherhood is called "virtuous." As peviously noted, this embraces several superlative qualities - "noble character," "capable," "perfect."
   2. Mothers are strategic forces (31:1-9).
      a. Lemuel is unknown. Probably an Arabian King or Chieftain. His adulthood was guided by his mother's influence.
      b. The King's mother followed a "strategy" in training her son. Counsel was given so the King would follow a certain course.
      c. Mothers occupy strategic roles in civilization's peaks and valleys.

      "The hand that rocks the cradle rules the world," women who are family-oriented will find out. Children raised in conservative homes are America's greatest asset for the future. Parents have the greatest power in influencing politics, values, and legislation for their childen. [Beverly LaHaye, ***Who Will Save Our Children,*** p. 233].

      d. Lemuel's mother trained her child with a strategy that focused upon the child's responsibility to live pure, recognize impropriety, respect laws, uphold justice, and actively pursue human dignity. America needs mothers today who will zealously follow this same strategy!
   3. Mothers have control of the family (31:18b).
      a. "Lamp" can suggest vigilance, watchfulness, or diligence regarding her family. If so, the mother was always alert and ready to act if danger was sensed.
      b. Other verses revealing this - 31:15,20,25,30.
   4. Mothers set the emotional tone in the home (31:25-29.)
      a. She has a good disposition, a sense of humor, optimism, and cheer (31:25b; 27:19).
      b. Kindness, not harsh, sarcastic jibs or nagging (31:26; 27:15).

c. The emphasis to mothers is verse 26 - speech habits are to reflect wisdom and kindness!
d. Imagine the home that is governed by a mother and wife with such (Titus 2:4,5).

5. Mothers must not yield to idleness (31:13-15).
   a. "Seeks" and "willingness" (13) describe her eagerness and delight in chores that benefit her family.
   b. "Rises" (15) describes her diligence.
   c. "Portion" (19) describes her organization in home's affairs.
6. This is a quick survey of the Bible's longest and best description of the mother.
   a. The importance of the mother in the home is well illustrated by Brenda Hunter in her outstanding book, ***"HOME BY CHOICE"*** (p. 93ff). Hunter discusses three feminists whose impact has changed society for the worse. These three, Betty Frieden, Germaine Greer, and Gloria Steinem were raised in homes where the mother's role was either missing or totally dysfunctional. They failed to receive the nurturing that Proverbs says must come from a caring mother. It is heartbreaking to read how these three were treated by their mothers. Listen to a few selected points. . .
      1) Regarding Betty Frieden, founder of the National Organization of Women - Her mother had "a complete inability to nurture. . .We really absolutely did not have a mother loving us." Her mother was intensely critical and made Betty feel unwanted and ugly.
      2) Germaine Greer describes her childhood as filled with pain and humiliation. Her mother viciously beat her. One day she opened the refrigerator to get a glass of milk and her mother said, "Leave that alone. That's for MY children." Her father "never once" hugged her.
      3) Gloria Steinem experienced a lack of parental love and nurture. Her father abandoned the family when she was eleven after her mother suffered a nervous breakdown. Her mother painted the windows of her house black and Steinem built emotional walls to guard against attachments.
      4) The consequences - Greer wrote that she "despised women." Steinem's absentee father led her to coin the pity slogan, "A woman needs a man like a fish needs a bicycle." There is a similarity in all radical feminist literature - the effect of a mother's absence upon her children! This is what Proverbs stresses! Hunter's conclusion is quite Scriptural - "Children, whether babies or teenagers, do not prosper when a mother is absent" (p. 100).
   b. Proverbs 14:1 - Such will build a STRONG FAMILY!
   c. 1 Peter 3:3-5 - Such will add beauty and value; true cosmetics!

III. The divine assurance (22:6). ***Transparency 2/6.***

A. Here is a command with a promise -
   1. The command - Train up a child in the right path.
   2. The promise - When old he will not depart from it.

B. There is much discussion regarding this text. Time will not allow a full discussion.
   1. Refer to lecture in 1992 Freed-Hardeman Lecture Book (p. 183ff) for full discussion of the major points in 22:6.
   2. We will briefly analyze the text.

C. Proverbs 22:6 analyzed.
   1. "Train" - to initiate or dedicate a child in a "way" that is right. This means. . .
      Parents must PLAN a child's training. Seldom is this done (Deuteronomy 6:6-9). In cases where a child's life was dedicated prior to birth, this promise was realized (i.e. Samuel - 1 Samuel 1:11; John - Luke 1:15b). Most parents plan for their child's educational, physical, and financial future - but few plan their spiritual! God's command is simple. Parents, before the child is born PLAN how you will train him/her!
   2. "Way" refers to the results of the training process.
      a. What kind of lifestyle do parents want children to live?
      b. There are 2 options - 15:9; 16:7.
      c. The "way" chosen must be lived by parents! (Genesis 18:19; Ephesians 6:4).
   3. "Should" refers to basic morality in life. Parents must talk to children about the nitty-gritty facts about life. Parents must speak from standards of absolutes in their own lives (1:8).
   4. "Will not depart" - A child whose parents have, from conception, planned, taught, and lived godly principles, will rejoice in a child who follows right.
      a. Such training can be spurned (3:1; 10:1).

b. Parents must fulfill their duty to this "training" process. That requires knowledge, wisdom, time spent with family, patience, determination, and love.
c. This process never ends (Job 1:5).
d. Time will quickly come when our children are no longer under our roof. At that point, may we join Hannah in her resolute trust (1 Samuel 1:28).
e. Close session by reading the last paragraph of this lecture in the Lectureship Book (p. 184).

The FATHER'S Role In Parenting a Strong Family

He shows STRENGTH [17:6]

He is RESPONSIBLE [11:14,29]

He DISCIPLINES [10:13; 12:1; etc.]

He is SPIRITUAL [12:28; 6:20ff]

He leaves INHERITANCE [13:22]

He provides STRENGTH IN TROUBLED TIMES [24:10]

[Transparency 2/1]

THE FATHER'S PUNISHMENT

According to Proverbs the father MUST discipline children. The reasons are clear . . .

1. **Neglect brings rebellion [13:24].**

2. **Such will save [6:23].**

3. **Such reveals parental love [3:11,12].**

[Transparency 2/2]

Father's Agenda

The Strong Family has a father who talks to his children about life's matters. He is specific and certain regarding instruction/caution to the child.

Friends
[22:24-26]

Sexuality
[6:25-29]

Priorities
[3:5,6,9,10]

Finances
[6:1-5]

Work Ethics
[6:6]

Decisions in everyday living
[7:4]

[Transparency 2/3]

WOMEN Described In Proverbs

Throughout Proverbs women are described in positive terms. The following facts are found.

Uniquely created to nurture, bear, and raise children.

Womanhood is exalted.

Men are to honor women.

What are celebrated . . . in these sayings are the grace and graciousness of womanhood and the marvelous contribution that an inwardly lovely woman makes to the building of a stable family. {Hubbard, p. 424, Commentary on Proverbs}

[Transparency 2/4]

BIBLICAL FEMININITY
In Proverbs

Various aspects of femininity are found in the marvelous Proverbs 31. These traits will assure strength in the family. All wives/mothers should strive to instill these points.

Motherhood is an honored role! [31:10]

Mothers are strategic people! [31:1-9]

Mothers have control of the family's morality, conscience, & welfare! [31:18b]

Mothers set the home's emotional tone! [31:25-29]

Mothers must not yield to idleness! [31:13-15]

[Transparency 2/5]

The Promise of Parenting
Proverbs 22:6

Here is a command and a promise that has caused much debate in study and heartache in life. Analyze its main points.

TRAIN
To initiate, dedicate. It refers to a determined plan. {cf. Deuteronomy 6:4ff; 1 Samuel 1:11; Luke 1:18b}

WAY
This is the result of the training. {cf. Proverbs 15:9; 16:7}

SHOULD
Refers to one's standard of decision-making.

WILL NOT DEPART
The consequence of a godly heart following godly training. {cf. Proverbs 3:1; 10:1}

[Transparency 2/6]

The Family's Fruits — Children

John L. Kachelman, Jr.

I. This lesson looks at the undergirding purpose of Proverbs. The book was written because children were valued and the parents wanted the child to develop healthy attitudes and practices in adult life. Solomon, Hezekiah's scribes, the anonymous wise men of chapters 22-24, Agur, and King Lemuel unite in declaring the sanctity of children and the responsiblity of parents to train their children.

Transparency 3/1 - A survey of the Proverbs that address children will divide itself into 4 parts.

1. There is great JOY in parenting.
2. There is great RESPONSIBILITY in training a child.
3. There is great URGENCY in the discipline of a child.
4. There is great RESPECT that must be instilled in a child. Look at each point in detail.

II. THE JOY! *(Transparency 3/2)*

A. The Holy Scriptures depict children in grand terms. They are treasures, gifts, and blessings sent from Jehovah God (cf. Psalms 127:3-5).

B. Proverbs looks at this joy from another angle - joy comes when the child behaves maturely and responsibly

1. This is a joy of satisfaction/reward. This joy gives birth to parental pride in the child's accomplishments and godly life.
2. The parental joy described in Proverbs arises from two actions.
   a. ***Wise Choices*** in daily life (23:15,16,24,25; 27:11). **23:16** "right things" suggests ethical integrity. The "heart" (v. 15) refers to the child's thought processes - they are right; "lips" refers to the child's manner of speech - it too is right. The parent who is confident of his child's thoughts and speech possesses great joy (v. 24,25). The agony of parents is to the same degree, only in reverse (10:1).
   b. ***Cooperative Obedience*** with God's will. The contrast in 13:22 is between fathers and children who either obey God or reject Him. There is great joy in the heart of a grandparent whose godliness has been passed down the family line. Pride and thanksgiving are abundant in them. But the family who lacks righteousness will find abject failure!

III. THE TRAINING *(Transparency 3/3)*

A. Proverbs was written specifically as a training manual for child-rearing. Here is the Lord's "How To Raise A Family" guidelines.

1. A point already made [in Study #2] is that children will follow some kind of training plan (22:6, Ephesians 6:4). Parents must consciously train children so they will grow in the "right" way.
2. ***Transparency 3/3a*** - The inspired training process mandates that parents train their children along these principles. . .
   a. Train them to listen to parental instruction (1:8; 2:1; 3:1; 6:20; 7:2,3; 10:1; 15:5,31,32; 19:20; 23:22).
   b. Teach them to honor the marriage covenant (2:17,18; 5:15-20; 6:27,32).
   c. Caution them to remember the "harvest" (5:21-23; 7:23; 11:19-21,29; 14:13; 17:3; 21:15; 22:8,9; 24:29).
   d. Teach them to choose the right priorities in life (8:5-11,18-21; 11:23-28; 23:4).
   e. Teach them to be open to correction (9:7-12; 10:17; 12:1).
   f. Train them to be diligent in work (10:4,5; 13:4,11; 20:4,13; 21:6,17; 21:25; 22:29).
   g. Develop self-discipline in them (16:32; 21:23; 23:26-28; 25:16).
   h. Show them that righteous living brings self-esteem (19:8; 20:11; 21:21).
   i. Forewarn them about alcoholic drinks (20:1; 23:29-35).
   j. Explain that greatness is gained only with humility (26:6,7; 26:12; 27:2,21; 29:23).

B. ***Transparency 3/3*** - Quickly discuss each point. Make brief references to passages with these points.

1. Clear-cut choices - Parents need to show children that absolute choices do appear. "Wise" counsel will help the child avoid "folly"! It is either God or Satan! Parents must make sure the child shoulders his/her responsibilities in making choices (cf. 1:32,33). Far too many delinquent children are allowed to escape the responsibility for their choices!
2. Past experiences of the child's peers ought to be used to illustrate wisdom and folly. Incidental anecdotes from daily life (cf. 26:3) speed this training process.
3. "Reasoning" parents help the child understand the need to make wise choices.
4. "Logic" - America is plagued with lazy thinkers. Children ought to be encouraged to think logically about the end of a choice (Proverbs 22:3).
5. Expect! Do not give rules without follow-up. Do not threaten unless prepared to act. Do not repeat over and over unless you want to train your children not to listen.
6. Parental experiences help the child see parents as "real" (4:3ff; 7:6ff).
7. Cause-and-Effect - Children need to learn about consequential results. Today most do not learn until too late that every action has consequences! (Galatians 6:7-8).

C. The training process is crucial! Parents who do not map out a proactive plan will find distressing regret (Lamentations 1:9).

IV. *The Discipline - Transparency 3/4*

A. Here is a topic urgently needed by today's parents. Proverbs is a rich resource for parents who are struggling with how they are to discipline a child.

B. There are 5 general points into which the Proverbs discussing discipline may be grouped.

1. ***The Reasons for Discipline*** are stated (***Transparency 3/4a***). **Note 4 Good Reasons to Discipline -**
   a. To remove foolishness (22:15). "Foolishness" refers to behavior that is rude, disrespectful, and irreverent. A child's action that reflects a lack of good judgement and respect must be met with stern measure.
   b. To rescue from Judgement (23:13,14). Parental duty is reflected by the emphatic "YOU"! Uncorrected behavior will lead a child to a life with early death.
   c. To impart wisdom (29:15). How many of us have heard parents gravely announce, "Now, I'm going to teach YOU a lesson!"? Wisdom is gained in many ways, and the "rod" is recommended by Solomon. A child without this ("left to himself;" "gets his own way" NASB) fails to develop proper behavior.
   d. To relieve anxiety (29:17). Two positive results are found in parental discipline: **"rest"** from worry, anxiety, and shame; **"delight"** in the joy of a good child.
2. ***The Purpose of Discipline:*** The singular objective is to make the child "wise" - to equip him with knowledge to succeed in life (22:5).
   a. **"Perverse"** - those deliberately wayward.
   b. The one who has been disciplined **"guards"** his entire life - physically, morally, and spiritually. He has learned to keep "far" from evil.
3. ***The Neglect of Discipline*** will bring three great tragedies.
   a. Such a parent **"hates"** the child - cares little about his future (13:24).
   b. Such a parent will grieve in bitter shame (29:15b). See Eli's tragic neglect and its consequences (1 Samuel 2:12,17,22-25,29).
   c. Such a parent **"trains"** a child in immorality (22:15a).
4. ***The Means of Discipline*** are clearly described.
   a. Parents are urged to use the **"rod"** (20:30; 23:13b).
   b. Parents are urged to use reproof (29:15).
   c. Parents are told to spank the child's "bottom" (10:13; 19:29; 26:3). Abuse is NOT sanctioned by God.
5. ***The Consistency of Discipline*** must be maintained. Inconsistent discipline is frustrating to the child. Prompt, immediate, and consistent discipline is needed (13:24).

V. The Respect Required in children (***Transparency 3/5***). The shameful actions of children will receive a tragic fate. Shameful, dishonorable children are addressed in 4 points.

A. The pain that dishonor brings (17:21,25).

B. The means of private dishonor (19:26; 20:20).

C. The embarrassment of public dishonor (28:7; 29:3).

D. The shame of misusing one's inheritance (17:2).

VI. *Transparency 3/6*

Proverbs tells how parents can lead a child to ruin. We must exercise wisdom's counsel if we want to have a STRONG FAMILY. Note these pitfalls -

A. Allow disrespect without correction (19:26; 20:20; 23:22; 28:24; 30:11,12,17).

B. Practice a lax discipline (13:24; 19:18; 6:32; 15:10; 23:13-16; 27:11).

C. Do nothing about a child's stubbornness (1:8,9; 4:1; 6:20-23; 13:1; 15:5; 19:13,26,27; 28:24).

D. Fail to develop discernment in the child (8:5-11,35-36; 9:17,18; 11:22; 14:7,12,15-18; 15:3; 16:17,25; 19:11; 23:4; 25:28; 28:7).

E. Encourage the child to have foolish friends (13:20; 22:24-25; 23:6,20-21; 24:21,22).

VII. *Transparency 3/7* - A program for parental instruction on how to train children about life will include these points.

A. ***Acknowledge*** that evil is surrounding us and will come into our children's lives. Do not ignore problems!

B. ***Awareness*** that our children are vulnerable to sin's temptation. Frankly discuss temptation's path.

C. ***Admit*** that past experiences equips parents to warn about the dangerous feelings, emotions, etc. Some children have a hard time conceiving of parents struggling with temptations.

D. ***Accept*** personal accountability - modern society encourages us to evade responsibility. Our failure to demand responsibility has resulted from the subtle changes in modern ethics. Modern man has been told that what is "natural" is not "wrong." Consequently, when one acts "naturally" s/he should not be subject to moral scrutiny. "After all, what moral judgement could be brought against a wolf that has killed a peasant's sheep; it was only doing what its nature demanded. Nature was natural, the naturalist said, and what was natural was good" [***Romanced to Death,*** p. 67ff]. This philosophy has affected the way parents train their children. A deplorable leniency has become the standard and "personal accountability" of the child has vanished.

E. ***Allow*** God's Scriptures to direct your parenting principles. Find total confidence in God's directions/standards/values.

The Family's Fruits—
♡CHILDREN♡

♡**The JOY. . .**

♡**The TRAINING. . .**

♡**The DISCIPLINE. . .**

♡**RESPECT REQUIRED IN. . .**

[Transparency 3/1]

THE JOY!

Comes from wise choices {27:11; 10:1; 15:20; etc.}

Comes from obedience to God {17:6; 13:22}

[Transparency 3/2]

The Training

Throughout Proverbs we find that a DELIBERATE program of training is urged for children {22:6; 23:12,19}. How?

Specific Instructions {1:8ff; 4:1ff; etc.}

Emphasize Child's Responsibility in Choices {1:32,33}

Use Past Experiences to Teach {3:5; 26:3}

Admonish with Reason {3:1b-2,13,14}

Encourage Logical Arguments {6:27; etc.}

Expect Obedience from Child {1:8; 4:1}

Reflect Upon Parental Experience {4:3ff}

Stress Cause-&-Effect {1:19; 6:24-33; etc.}

[Transparency 3/3]

Parental Training Includes. . .

The book of Proverbs commands parents to follow a process of parenting which includes training children in these areas:

Listen to parental instructions
{1:8; 2:1; 3:1; 6:20; 7:2,3; 10:1; etc.}

Honor the marriage commitment
{2:17,18; 5:15-20; 6:27,32}

Remember the "harvest"
{5:21-23; 7:23; 11:19-21,29; 14:13}

Choose right priorities
{8:5-11,18-21; 11:23-28; 23:4}

Teach them to be open to correction
{9:7-12; 10:17; 12:2}

Train diligence in work
{10:4,5; 13:4,11; 20:4,13; etc.}

Develop self-discipline in them
{16:32; 21:23; 23:26-27; 25:19}

Communicate benefits of righteousness
{19:8; 20:11; 21:21}

Warn about alcoholic drinks
{20:1; 23:29-35}

Teach that greatness comes via humility
{26:6,7,12; 27:2,21; 29:23}

[Transparency 3/3a]

The Discipline!

Proverbs is a rich resource manual regarding parental discipline. It teaches parents . . .

The Reasons . . .
{22:15}

The Purpose . . .
{22:5,6}

The Neglect of . . .
{13:24}

The Means . . .
{29:15}

The Consistency . . .
{13:24}

[Transparency 3/4]

Four Reasons for Discipline

To Remove "Foolishness"
Proverbs 22:15

To Impart Wisdom
Proverbs 29:15

To Relieve Anxiety
Proverbs 29:17

To Rescue from Judgement
Proverbs 23:13,14

[Transparency 3/4a]

The RESPECT Required In Children

Parents who fail to instill respect in a child will suffer . . .

Pain of dishonor {17:21,25}

Tolerance of private dishonor {19:26; 20:20}

Embarrassment of public dishonor {28:7; 29:3}

Shame of a misused inheritance {17:2}

[Transparency 3/5]

Leading a Child to Ruin!

Allow disrespect without correction
{19:26; 20:20; 23:22; 28:24; 30:11,12,17}

Practice lax discipline
{13:24; 19:18; 6:32; 15:10; 23:13-16; 27:11}

Ignore stubbornness
{1:8,9; 4:1; 6:20-23; 13:1; 15:5; 19:13,26,27; 28:24}

Fail to develop discernment
{8:5-11,35-36; 9:17,18; 11:22; 14:7,12,15-18; 15:3; 16:17,25; 19;11: 23:4, 25:28; 28:7}

Encourage foolish friendships
{13:20; 22:24-25; 23:6,20-21; 24:21,22}

[Transparency 3/6]

A Program for Parental Instruction Will:

ACKNOWLEDGE!

AWARENESS!

ADMIT

ACCEPT!

ALLOW!

[Transparency 3/7]

The Family's Filigree — Uniqueness

John L. Kachelman, Jr.

I. *Note:* The thoughts for point "I" were discovered while reading the excellent book, *The Child Influencers,* by Dan Adams.

June 17, 1943 - A 20 year old pilot starts the engine of his West Lysander on a runway in Sussex, England. At 2 o'clock in the morning, the sound of his engine pierces the lonely night. A single passenger climbs in and the plane rises heavily in the air. The aircraft, known as a moon plane, is painted a dull black, causing it to quickly disappear against the night sky. The pilot's destination: a quiet field near Le Mans in German-occupied France. His cargo: a striking young woman radio-telegraph operator in the French underground resistance. By pale moonlight the pilot flies low over the English Channel, then strains to see landmarks below. Finally, a prearranged pattern of lights on a deserted field comes into view, and he noses his plane down. In several minutes Madeleine will be making her way toward a railroad station, and he will be soaring back to England. {*From the true account of the British master spy, Sir Stephenson.* ***A Man Called Intrepid: The Secret War,*** *p. 235-256*}.

Imagine yourself in the cockpit, peering into near-blackness. How would you feel about navigating in the dark, surrounded by danger, and responsible for precious cargo? As a parent, that is exactly what we are doing!

On that dark night in 1943, the pilot successfully completed his mission because he was prepared [***Transparency 4/3***]. His success was due to his proficiency in using three vital tools:

1. Maps
2. Flight Instruments
3. Training Manual
4. ***Note:*** Parents also rely upon these 3 tools to give them safe delivery of children to adulthood [***Transparency 4/4***].
   a. Maps - Historical Truths
   Collective wisdom from experiences in the past. Parents have largely discarded this element and children in our modern times are being raised in a fashion unlike any other time. Parents today are not looking at the maps used by forefathers!
   b. Flight Instruments - Research Truths
   Behavior is often predictable. Studies enable parents to avoid catastrophe by revealing predictable patterns. But today's parents opt for ignorance of proven data and blindly trust in twisted reasoning.
   c. Training Manual - The Holy Scriptures
   Here is the most important tool. But this, the greatest of all three, is grossly ignored; its importance minimized. Today the Scriptures are discarded by parents and society alike!

II. There is one reoccurring fact throughout Proverbs - STRONG FAMILIES do not just happen, they are the consequence of planning and forethought! As such they are characterized by certain unique traits. These traits adorn the STRONG FAMILY just as intricately carved filigrees beautify buildings erected with painstaking care. Examine some of these decorative traits of a STRONG FAMILY.

A. Discussion of the list of traits associated with "Strong Families" [***Transparency 4/1***].
1. **Loyalty** - 17:17 "at all times" admits no exceptions.
2. **Reputation** - One's family will share some kind of reputation. The strong family's reputation is that of godliness. The tragedy of a bad reputation is as one famished being offered a feast only to have a tooth break. Or, to have palsy strike your foot before an important race (25:19). Cf. Ecclesiastes 7:1.
3. **Endurance** - 17:17a "all times"
4. **Dependence** - Strong families are so dependable in godliness that gossip does not diminish it.
5. **Accountability** - 27:17 cites the positive impact of family members being accountable to one another.

6. **Forgiveness** - 19:11, 24:17; 29,25:21 Strong Families are willing to forgive so mistakes lead to wisdoms lessons.
7. **Sensitivity** - 22:9 pronounces a "blessing" upon the sensitive heart. The family that is known for having a good "eye" (9a) is a blessing.
8. **Honesty** - 21:2 the family must practice the Lord's honest standard. Egyptian hieroglyphics pictured the human heart being weighed on the scale of balance with the feather of Truth.
9. **Reverence** - 20:25 cautions families against rash vows and impious promises. The verb used indicates wild promises made under pressure; a foxhole pledge that is later recanted ("reconsider").
10. **Contentment** - 19:1,22; 20:8-9. Strong Families have learned the wisdom of fleeing materialism's lure.
11. **Respect** - 23:22
12. **Communication** - 25:11. Through Proverbs the family is urged to communicate. *"My observation of strong families has convinced me that there is a high level of spontaneity in the communiction style. At times, it might be mistaken by an outsider as confusion"* [Royce Money, p. 38, ***Building Strong Families***].

B. ***Transparency 4/5*** - Strong Families are characterized by constant instruction of parents to children. (Proverbs 1:8; 4:1,10; 19:20; 8:6,33; 19:27; etc.).
1. This is in obedience to God (Deuteronomy 6:4-9). This duty was given to parents so children would be trained to be loyal to Jehovah instead of embracing ungodly lifestyles.
2. This constant instruction includes -
   a. Parents whose instructions are given to children in ways such as these:
      1) Diligently (7a)
      2) Continually (7b)
      3) Visibly (8; cf. Proverbs 7:3)
      4) Practically (9) - outside the home, parents are to show children that God's Word is still practiced!
3. A practical consequence of parental observance of Deuteronomy 6 - Parents have to be **WITH** their children a large part of the day! But most parents are not!
   a. Society discourages this by subtle messages of children being a nuisance, etc.
   b. Work discourages this by encouraging advancement; sponsored day care centers; etc.
   c. Families discourage this by allowing members to schedule activities that lead to a separation of the family unit.
   d. Families discourage this by television habits.

C. ***Transparency 4/6*** - Strong Families nurture self-esteem in members. From the treasures of Proverbs on families, come three specifics which parents must practice if they are to instill self-esteem in a child.
1. ***Proverbs 20:5 - An Insightful Understanding*** of the talents and abilities of each child. The wise parent will be the source of encouragement for the child and will be patient and probing to discover the hidden talents of a child. Sometimes this is a hard task, but the "understanding" parent will do it!
2. ***Proverbs 27:17 - An Involvement that Strengthens.*** There is no substitute for a child/parent interaction - nothing! The child's judgement is sharpened as his thoughts/ideas meet the parents'. Lest parents scoff - "Iron upon iron" - the same material can affect one another in a positive way!
3. ***Proverbs 27:19 - A Reasoned Reflection.*** Parents need to help the child see inner attitudes/emotions and counsel if these are wrong. Self-understanding in a child is enhanced by the caring parent as the parent "plays" back" the child's message. ***Note:*** As water reflects best when it is calm and still, so does the parent! ***Calm and still*** reasoning will help develop the child's understanding.

D. ***Transparency 4/7*** - Strong Families portray a genuine "love" for children. Psalms 127,128 were authored by Solomon. Notice the emphasis he gives upon the family. Four metaphors are used in regard to children:
1. ***Children are a GIFT*** (3a).
   The Hebrew root means "property" or "possession." Hence, children are given to parents as "property" on loan from God.
2. ***Children are a REWARD*** (3b).
   They reward the loving commitment between man and woman. They are a trophy of loving trust.
3. ***Children are like ARROWS*** (4-5).
   "Arrows" portray strength and security. Such are children (1 Timothy 5:4). But an arrow in battle is only good if it has been skillfully fashioned. An arrow is also good only to the one who uses it with skill and strength!

4. ***Children are an OLIVE PLANT*** (128:1-3).
   A beautiful setting; perfectly arranged; diligently nurtured; possesses life and blessings.
5. The parents' chore -
   a. **Be Thankful** for the gift - their attitudes should reveal this marvelous gift.
   b. **Honor** the reward - awards ought to be honored with satisfaction. Children today are seldom "prized."
   c. **Fashion** the arrow - how are you preparing your child?
   d. **Dress and tend** the olive plants - encouragement and discipline are essential. They are to be pruned with the tenderness of a caring vinedresser so they will be productive in life!

E. ***Transparency 4/8*** - Strong Families guard against rebellion. The tragedy of Eli's family must be avoided. This can be done if we recognize where he went "wrong" in parenting (cf. 1 Samuel 2:11-3:13).
1. ***Children did not know the Lord*** (2:12).
   They missed this vital aspect of life! Apparently Eli was too busy to be involved with his sons' religious training.
2. ***Parents tolerated fleshly sin in children*** (2:22).
3. ***Parents failed to apply corrective discipline*** (2:23-25a).
4. ***Parents failed to teach respect*** (2:25b).
5. ***Parents failed to develop the children's submissiveness*** (3:11-13). "Rebuke" (13) root means to grow weak. Eli did nothing to weaken the attitudes and rebellious wills of his sons!

III. Concluding Observations.

Transparency 4/2 - Use this to summarize the general thoughts of the study series.

THE STRONG FAMILY'S FILIGREE!

☞ **Loyalty** {3:3,4; 17:6}

Reputation ☜ {12:26; 19:22}

☞ **Endurance** {17:17; 24:19}

Dependence ☜ {25:10}

☞ **Accountability** {12:15; 17:10}

Forgiveness ☜ {10:12; 16:6}

☞ **Sensitivity** {14:21-23}

Honesty ☜ {14:25}

☞ **Reverence** {14:26; 16:3,20}

Contentment ☜ {30:8,9}

☞ **Respect** {16:31}

Communication ☜ {25:11}

[Transparency 4/1]

How Does the STRONG FAMILY Stay Together?

LOVE for the Spiritual!

DISCIPLINE from concern!

CONSISTENCY providing security!

EXAMPLE instilling faith/commitment

A MAN AS THE HEAD who places God top priority!

[Transparency 4/2]

Success Depends on 3 Vital Tools

MAPS

FLIGHT INSTRUMENTS

TRAINING MANUAL

[Transparency 4/3]

Effective Tools for Parents

Maps —
Historical Truths!

Flight
Instruments —
Research Truth!

Training Manual —
The Holy Scriptures!

[Transparency 4/4]

STRONG FAMILIES —
Constant Instruction
{cf. Proverbs 1:8; 4:1; 19:20; etc.}

Note these specific points from Deuteronomy 6:4-9

Parents whose faith is secure (6:4,5)

Parents whose instructions are given

a. DILIGENTLY (7a)
b. CONTINUALLY (7b)
c. VISIBLY (8; cf. Proverbs 7:3)
d. PRACTICALLY (9)

[Transparency 4/5]

STRONG FAMILIES
Nurture Self-Esteem

AN INSIGHTFUL UNDERSTANDING
{Proverbs 20:5}

INVOLVEMENT THAT STRENGTHENS
{Proverbs 27:17}

A REASONED REFLECTION
{Proverbs 27:19}

[Transparency 4/6]

STRONG FAMILIES
Portray Genuine LOVE!

Psalms 127, 128 were authored by Solomon. His "wise" counsel for building STRONG FAMILIES is reflected in these passages. Four metaphors suggest the attitude of parents toward children . . .

Children Are Like A(n) . . .

- ☺ **GIFT (3a)**
- ☺ **REWARD (3b)**
- ☺ **ARROW (4,5)**
- ☺ **OLIVE PLANT (128:1-3)**

[Transparency 4/7]

STRONG FAMILIES
Guard Against Rebellion!

The tragedy of Eli's family will be avoided by families today. This can be done by avoiding the tragic parent/child relationship we find in this tale. {*See 1 Samuel 2:11-3:13*}

Children did not know God (2:12).

Parents tolerated child's sin (2:22).

Parents failed to discipline (2:23-25a).

Parents failed to instill respect (2:25b).

Parents failed to develop submissiveness (3:11-13)

[Transparency 4/8]

Short Sketches from Proverbs

John L. Kachelman, Jr.

The Purposes of Scripture (1:1-6)

a. To provide **knowledge** - "to know."
b. To lead to **discernment** - "to discern."
c. To **mature** - "to receive."
d. To **enlighten** - "to give."

WHO is a Wise Man? (1:5)

"Wisdom" is pursued by many who fail to understand its true nature. Solomon's words describe such for us.

a. He "hears" - has an open mind to reason.
b. He "increases" - always advancing; progressive.
c. He "acquires counsel" - is open to other's ideas/thoughts.
d. He has "will" - the desire/motivation to do.

The Way of the Fool (1:22-23)

a. A total rejection of God (24,25).
b. Hopelessness when in trouble (26-28).
c. Foolish folly will be met with Divine wrath (29-31).
d. The broad way leading to destruction (32).

Wonderful Peace! (1:33)
The blessed peace described here is a wonderful gift. Many are seeking it today. Note some facts about it.
a. It begins with listening to God.
b. It provides secure living.
c. It yields a contented "ease."
d. It overcomes "dread of evil."

The Contrast of Lifestyles (Proverbs 1)
In life we see a dramatic contrast between the wise and the foolish. Actions, language, and outcome are all different. Note how Solomon draws this contrast in chapter one.
a. Contrast between life's objectives (1-6,13,22).
b. Contrast in their response to advice (5,8,24,25).
c. Contrast in the way God is viewed (7).
d. Contrast in friends/associates (10).
e. Contrast in how earthly trials are met (25-28,33).
f. Contrast in eternal fate (31-33).

Godly Preserves (2:8-11)
God preserves His saints as if they are gathered behind a great shield. How can we be shielded by God?
a. Through discernment (9).
b. Through wisdom (10a).
c. Through knowledge (10b).
d. Through discretion (11a).

e. Through understanding (11b).
f. These will bring a harvest of pleasing fruits: "good," "pleasant," "guard," "watch."

The Key to Popularity (3:4)

a. Respect parental guidelines (3:1).
b. A determination to be honest and kind (3:3).
c. Desire to follow God before man (3:4,5).

Success Spelled by God (3:13-18)

There are all kinds of formulas for finding success. But only one promises genuine success. The way of "wisdom" will yield a success unsurpassed. Those who find wisdom, also find. . .

a. Long Life (16a).
b. Riches and Honor (16b).
c. Pleasant Ways (17a).
d. Peace (17b).
e. Lasting Happiness (18).

Counsel for Life (3:5-8)

a. For uncertainties - "Trust in the Lord" (5).
b. For choices - "In all ways acknowledge Him" (6).
c. For values - "do not be wise in own eyes" (7).
d. For satisfaction - "healing to your body" (8).

Materialism Controlled by Generosity (3:5-9)
a. The Attitude - "Honor the Lord."
b. The Gift - "From your wealth."
c. The Priority - "First."
d. The Reason - "Trust in the Lord."

Godly Rewards (3:1-26)
Throughout the passage, Solomon urges godliness because of the rewards that such would bring.
a. Obedience to parental advice brings a good life (1-4).
b. Obedience to divine will brings satisfaction in life (5-10).
c. Obedience to the Lord's chastening brings security (11-12).
d. Obedience to wisdom brings happiness (13-26).

A Father's Confidence (4:1-4)
a. Confident in his role to advise (1).
b. Confident in the value of his counsel (1b-2a).
c. Confident in the necessity of his teaching (2b).
d. Confident due to prior training (3-4).

Essential Acquisitions (4:5)
a. Acquire WISDOM for it will guard your heart (2:10a; 3:21,22).
b. Acquire UNDERSTANDING for it will lead you to pleasantness (2:10b,11; 1:33; 4:13).
c. The imperative for these - 4:7b - "with all" (2:2-6).

A Foolish Lifestyle (4:10-19)

The fool rejects God's wisdom and is devoted to selfishness. The calamity awaiting is thus described. . .

a. They will be "impeded" - always troubled (12).
b. They will be addicted to evil (16.)
c. They will be filled with wickedness (17.)
d. They will live in darkness (19).

The Path of the Righteous (4:18)

a. It is like "light" - exposes the right, confronts the wrong.
b. It increases - growth and maturity are evident.
c. It continues "until" the brightness of Heaven arrives.

The Path of the Wicked (4:19)

a. It is "darkness" - ignorant, lost, and unable to lead.
b. It is guided by ignorance - "They do not know." Such have chosen not to discover God's wisdom.
c. It culminates in "stumbling" - they will fall, unable to rise. They are without hope of strength.

Practical Counsel (4:24-27)

a. Watch the way you speak (24).
b. Keep your eyes focused on God's Will (25).
c. Follow the path of the righteous (26; cf. 4:18-19).
d. Be determined in living life (27).

Better than Silver or Gold! (4:13-26)

To a materialistic world such sounds absurd. What could be better than our precious metals?

a. The better "commodity" - WISDOM!

b. The better "riches" - "BLESSED" indicates that these are much better because of the results obtained: long life; honor; pleasantness; peace; happiness.

c. The better "rationale" - Why one should do this is fully explained. Wisdom and understanding are only able to provide man the security he seeks (19-26).

Conversion Simplified (3:7-8)

a. The Command - "Fear the Lord" (cf. Acts 2:37; 16:29-30).

b. The Action - "Turn away from it" (cf. Acts 2:38; 3:19).

c. The Result - "Healing and Refreshment" (Acts 3:19; 16:34).

Guidelines for a Sound Marriage (Misc. Proverbs)

a. Recognize the responsibility of each (14:1).

b. Discretion will guard (11:22; 12:4).

c. Harmony should reign (21:9,19; 25:24; 27:15,16).

d. Integrity should be foremost (22:14).

e. Honor should overwhelm materialism (11:16).

Why Listen to Parents? (1:5,7,8; 30:17)

a. Because honor is given to parents (23:22,25).

b. Because their teaching is reliable (3:3; 8:7, 18:15).
c. Obedience brings continual joy (2:20).

Guidelines for a Child's Discipline (Misc. Proverbs)

Depending upon the discipline of parents, their children will be a source of either joy or sorrow (29:15,17). Here are some godly guidelines for disciplining your children so joy will be a part of your home.

a. Define boundaries of accepted/unaccepted behavior before they must be enforced. Make instructions clear.
b. Enforce boundaries when they are violated. Be consistent.
c. Discipline in private to avoid unnecessary embarrassment.
d. Discipline with a neutral object (i.e. "rod"). Cf. 10:13; 13:24; 14:3; 22:8,15; 23:13,14; 26:3; 29:15.
e. Discipline remembering that your child is created in God's image and deserves dignified treatment - no cruel "put downs" or sadistic, humiliating punishment.
f. Remain in control. Do not lash out in anger! Do not discipline when fatigued.

Basics of Child Training (22:6)

a. The NATURE of training - "Train up" comes from the action of the mid-wife who would dip her fingers into the juice of crushed dates and then massage the gums of the newborn to create a sensation of sucking. The babe would then be given to the mother to nurse. Thus, parents should instill a "desire" within the child for what is "wise."

b. The DURATION of the training - from the time s/he is a "child" to when "old." The training process is for the entire time the child is under parental care.

c. The IMPLEMENTATION of the training - "in." Parents must begin immediately to point the child in godly "ways." Those who wait will regret their delay!

Love Makes a House a Home! (Misc. Proverbs)

a. Proverbs 10:12 - love seeks to resolve conflict without strife.

b. Proverbs 13:24 - love is diligent in keeping the home godly.

c. Proverbs 15:17 - a loving home is valuable and treasured.

The Worthy Woman - General Traits (Proverbs 31:10ff)

a. She is "worthy" - possessing strength of character, morality, and righteousness.

b. She is "trustworthy" (11) - her husband can trust her with anything: his name, children, business, honor, etc.

c. She is "good" (12) - a good helper for she always is looking out for his interests; a good mother for she provides what her children need; a good citizen for she lives a respectable and kind life; a good employer for she is considerate of those working for her.

The Worthy Woman - Specifics (Proverbs 31:10ff)

a. Willing (13-15)

b. Financially responsible (16)

c. Strong (17)
d. Appreciative (18a)
e. Vigilant (18b)
f. Skillful in home matters (19)
g. Charitable (20)
h. Confident (21)
i. Attractive (22)
j. Good for husband (23)
k. Wise (26-29)
l. Has high values (24,25)

Bibliography for Resources

Adams, Dan. ***The Child Influencers,*** Home Team Press: Cuyahoga Falls, Ohio, 1990.

Building Stronger Christian Families. **Freed-Hardeman University 1992 Lectures.** Freed-Hardeman University, Henderson, TN, 38340-2399, 1992. **Note:** This entire lectureship book is devoted to a Scriptural study of the family. Audio tapes of each lecture are available from the University's bookstore (901-989-6000).

Glenn, H. Stephen & Jane Nelson. ***Raising Self-Reliant Children in a Self-Indulgent World,*** Prima Publishing & Communications, P.O. Box 1260SR, Rocklin, CA 95677; (916) 624-5718, 1989.

Gore, Tipper. ***Raising PG Kids in an X-Rated Society,*** Abingdon Press, Nashville, 1987.

deParrie, Paul. ***Romanced to Death: The Sexual Seduction of American Culture,*** Wolgemuth & Hyatt, Publishers, Inc., Brentwood, TN, 1989.

Dobson, Dr. James. ***Hide or Seek: How to Build Self-Esteem in Your Child,*** Fleming Revell Co., Old Tappan NJ, 1974.

Hocking, David. ***Moral Catastrophe: The Future Survival of the American Family,*** Harvest House Pub., Eugene, OR, 1990.

Hunter, Brenda. ***[Facing the effects of mother's absence] Home by Choice: Creating Emotional Security in Children,*** Multnomah, Portland, OR 1991.

LaHayne, Beverly. ***Who Will Save Our Children? "30 Strategies for Protecting Your Child from a Threatening World."*** Wolgemuth & Hyatt, Pub., Inc. Brentwood, TN 1990.

Marshner, Connie, ***Can Motherhood Survive?*** Wolgemuth & Hyatt, Pub., Inc. Brentwood, TN 1990.

Marshner, Connie. ***How to Teach Your Children About Sex: DECENT EXPOSURE.*** Wolgemuth & Hyatt Pub., Inc. Brentwood, TN 1988.

Money, Royce. ***Building Stronger Families.*** Victor Books: Wheaton, IL 1984.